Piano Vocal Guitar

The LAST SONG

Music from the Motion Picture Soundtrack

ISBN 978-1-4234-9575-8

BUENA VISTA MUSIC COMPANY

DISTRIBUTED BY

HAL•LEONARD®
CORPORATION
7777 W. BLUEMOUND RD. P.O. BOX 13819 MILWAUKEE, WI 53213

Visit Hal Leonard Online at
www.halleonard.com

Due to licensing restrictions, "Down the Line"
and "Each Coming Night" are not included in this folio.

TYRANT

Words and Music by RYAN TEDDER,
ANDREW JOHN BROWN and ZACH FILKINS

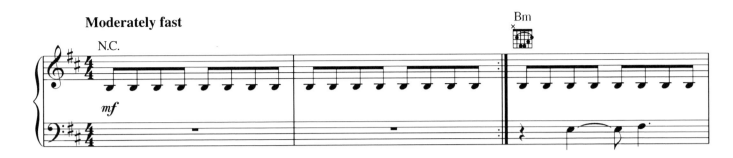

Watch - in' my - self,___ and I'm tak - ing strides,___

but here comes the moon, and it feels and it feels like an in- form-

-er. Quick, run a-way, hide be- fore they see you. You know it is all,

all a- glow.

Bm

Walk- ing on wa- ter seems per- il- ous now. You've got my trust,

ty - rant.

Bm

Ca - pa - ble of ____ 'most an - y - thing, ___ this crip - pled bird's _

_ gon - na sing, _ gon - na bring __ you all the an - swers. Turn a - round and

look. Your shad-ow's cook - in' up beau - ti - ful lies _____ for

you. It's what _____ they do. And it feels _____

D.S. al Coda

Gmaj7#4   Gmaj7

CODA

from the out, _____ from the out, _

A6/9   Bm/A   Bm11

ty - rant. _____

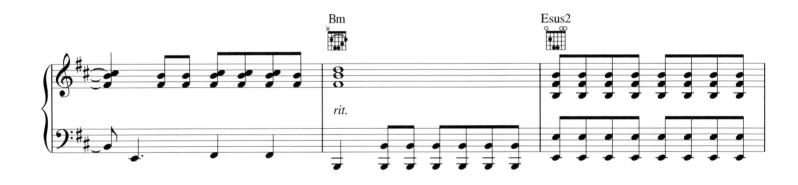

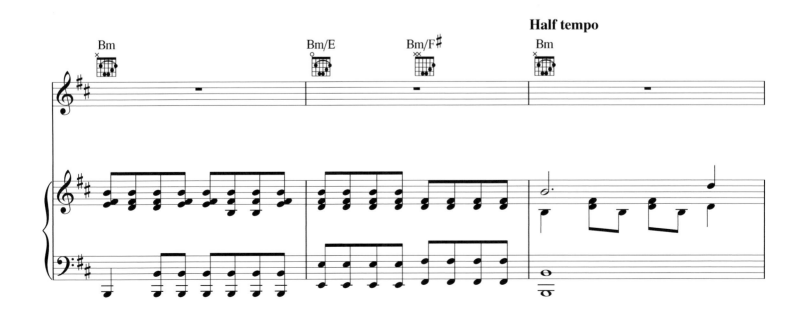

jus - ti - fy _____ me. _____

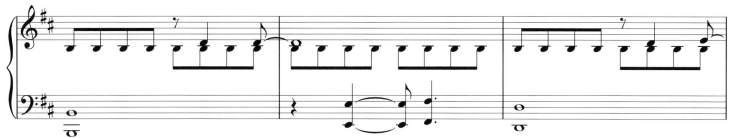

From the out, __

from the out, __

from the out, __ and it feels __ so __ real __

from the out - side look - ing in. __

BRING ON THE COMETS

Words and Music by MARK GUIDRY,
MARK PALGY and CRAIG PFUNDER

SETTING SUN

Words and Music by STUART MACLEOD,
JOEL QUARTERMAIN and FINLAY BEATON

Moderate Modern Rock

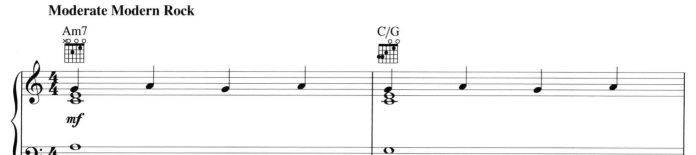

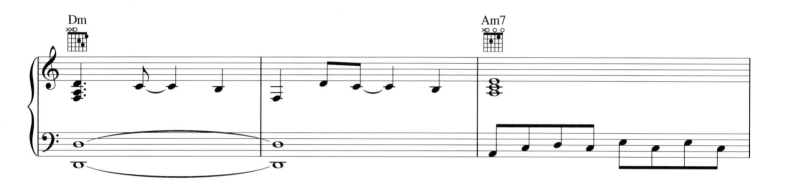

I've been wait - ing for too long, star - ing at the sun.

Ice is just a rem - e - dy for pain and ris - ing heat.

vocal 1st time only

And if I see you wait-ing for the set-ting sun, _____ it will nev-er _____ come. _____ And if it ev-er comes, _

you're for - ev - er young, _____ you're for - ev - er _____ young. _____

WHEN I LOOK AT YOU

Words and Music by JOHN SHANKS
and HILLARY LINDSEY

BROOKLYN BLURS

Words and Music by ALEX WONG
and DEVON COPLEY

Moderate Acoustic Folk

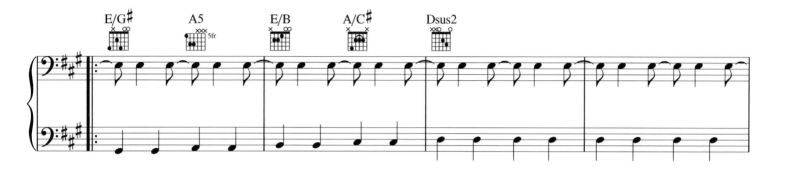

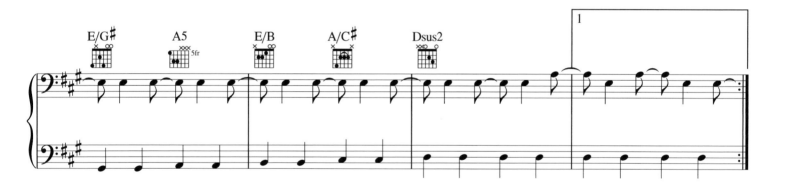

I took the N Train
Be - tween mis - takes and

CAN YOU TELL

Words and Music by WES MILES, MATHIEU SANTOS,
MILO BONACCI, ALEXANDRA LAWN,
REBECCA ZELLER and JOHN PIKE

I HOPE YOU FIND IT

Words and Music by STEVE ROBSON
and JEFFREY STEELE

These clouds aren't go-ing no - where, ba - by,
"Am I sup-posed to hang a-round and wait for - ev - er?"

rain keeps com-ing down. _____
Last words that I said. _____

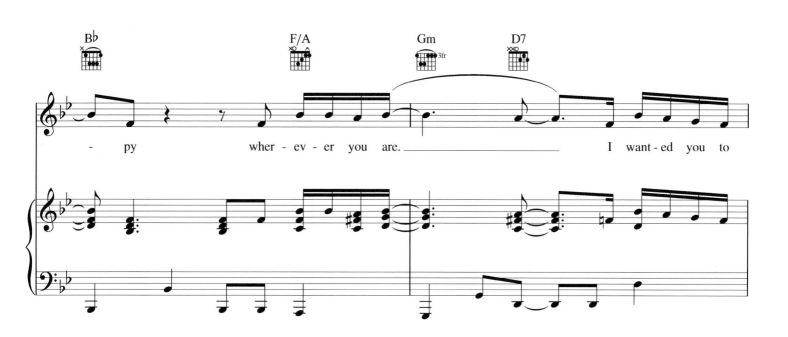

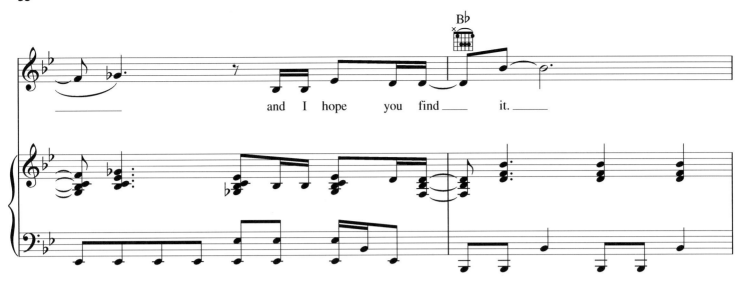

and I hope you find ___ it. ___

I hope you find ___ it. ___ Mmm. ___

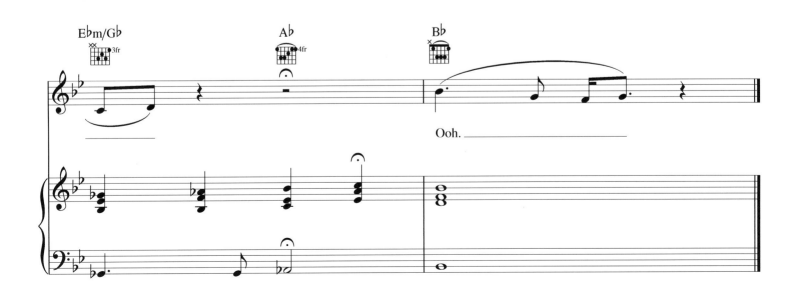

Ooh. ___

SHE WILL BE LOVED

Words and Music by ADAM LEVINE
and JAMES VALENTINE

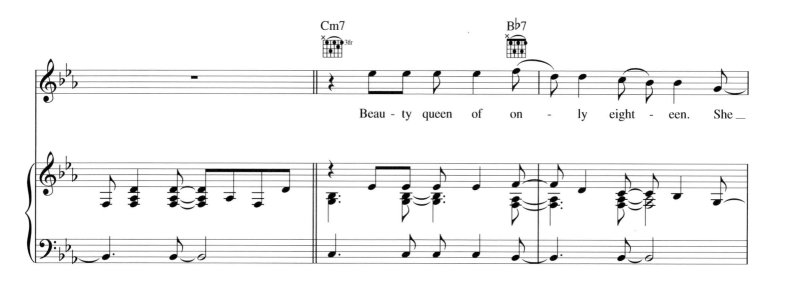

Beau-ty queen of on - ly eight - een. She __

__ had some trou-ble with __ her - self. __ He was al-ways there __

NEW MORNING

Words and Music by
CASEY McPHERSON

Moderate Modern Rock

mf   *sim.*

I don't give a damn__ a-bout the cas-tle on__ the hill, or the gold__

__ that we__ could eat, or the horse__ you have__ for sale. No, I'm

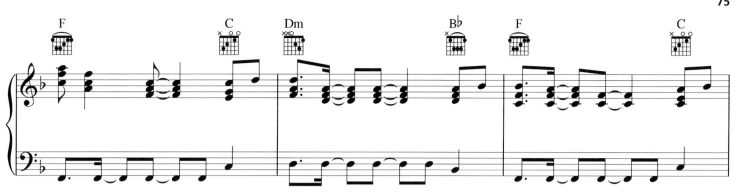

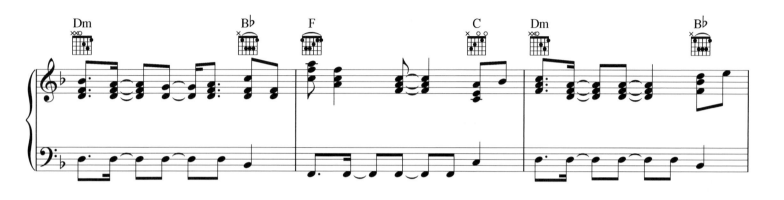

D.S. al Coda

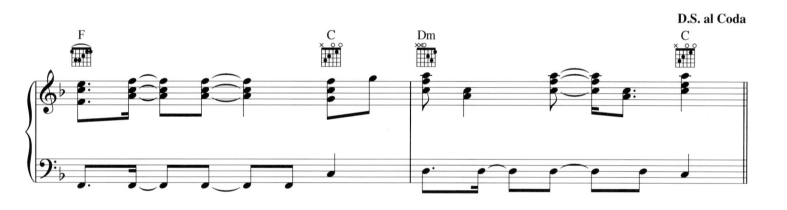

CODA

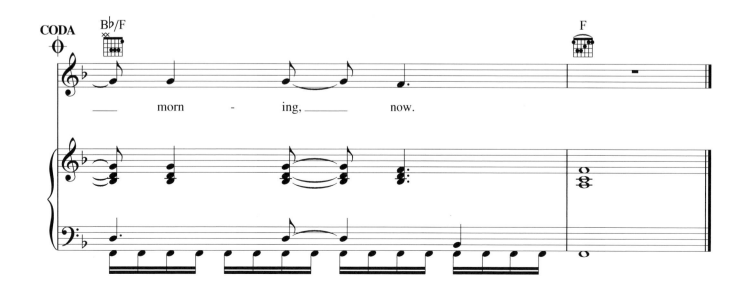

___ morn - ing, ___ now.

BROKE DOWN HEARTED WONDERLAND

Words and Music by MAIA SHARP,
EDWIN McCAIN, PETE RILEY
and KEVIN KINNEY

Broke down heart - ed won - der - land. _____

vocal 1st time only

sax solo 1st time, guitar solo on repeat

A DIFFERENT SIDE OF ME

Words and Music by NATHAN DARMODY,
ZACHARY PORTER and TOM NORRIS

NO MATTER WHAT

Words and Music by SYDNEE DURAN
and DAVE BASSETT

HEART OF STONE

Words and Music by
SUNE ROSE WAGNER

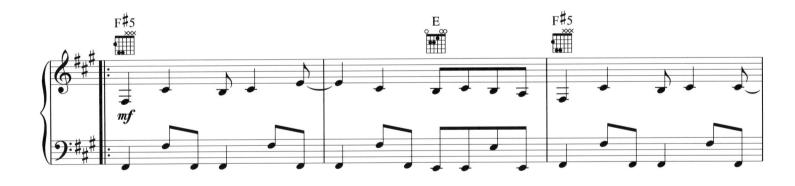

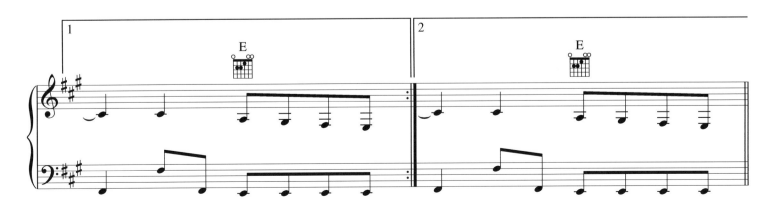

I've got a heart of stone. ___

guitar solo

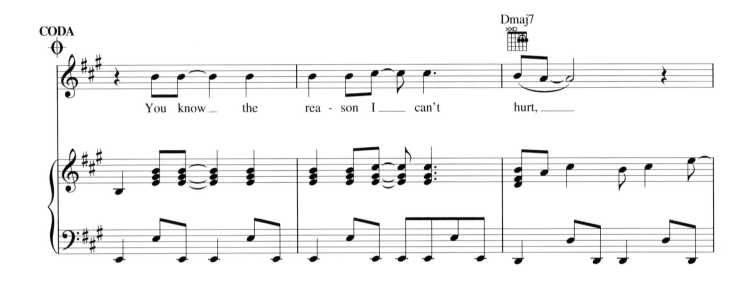

STEVE'S THEME

Music by AARON ZIGMAN

Slowly, with rubato

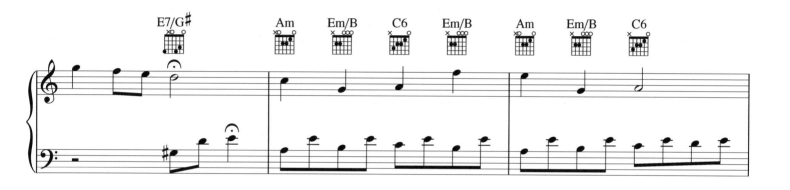

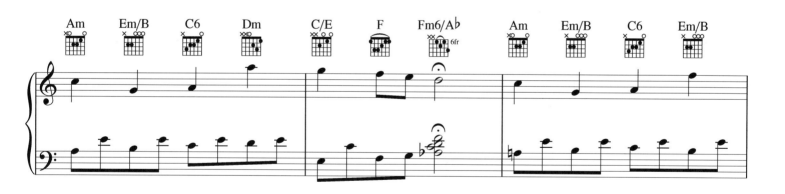

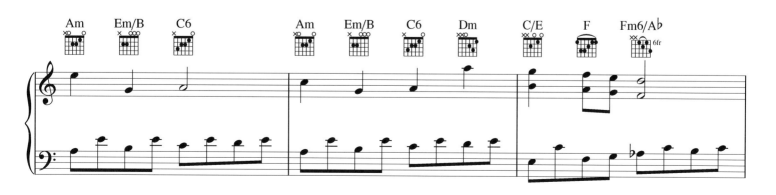